Bed of Crimson Joy

Bed of Crimson Joy

Joan Lauri Poole

carrytiger

New York • New York

Copyright © 2012 Joan Lauri Poole

Cover/interior design: Nancy Figueiredo

Cover painting: Rembrandt Harmensz van Rijn (1606–1669). "Bathseba in the bath." 1654. Oil on canvas, 142 x 142 cm. Louvre, Paris, France

Photo credit: Erich Lessing / Art Resource, NY

Cover background photograph: Shutterstock.com

Author photograph © John Couturier

Drawing on page 77 © Emma Riba

LIBRARY OF CONGRESS Control Number: 2011914495

Bed of crimson joy / by Joan Lauri Poole.

ISBN 978-0615-4547-40

Printed in the United States of America

987654321

First Edition

—William Blake

Contents

Backwards like the crab

Sister/3
Rembrandt's "Jewish Bride"/4
Bradford Pear Trees/5
The Urge to Pray in Bryant Park/6
The Journey Home/7
Transcendentalists/8
Jones Beach/9
Swinging/10
Foal Days/11
Adolescent Summer/12
Caught in Stone/13
Every Day/14
Remembering Susan/15
Leave-Taking/16
In the Bedroom Under the Bookshelves/17

Things—mutable as they are

Winter Light/21
Clear Night Outside Rite-Aid With Jupiter Overhead/22
Music/23
Hermes/24
Queen Anne's Lace/26
The Cockscomb/27
The Camaraderie of Frogs/28
The Cerebellum Singing Its Cosmic Scales/29
Clark Gardens/30
By the Sound/31
Hummingbird Haiku/32

Masculine / Feminine

Love-Charm Song/35
Floating Dream/36
Things That Aren't There/37
For Vermeer and His "Sleeping Girl"/38
The New Room/39
Orchidelirium/40
Subway Flowers/41
The Tightrope Walker Whose Wire Is Herself/42
Virgin/43
Panic/44
Dear Anger/45
Un/46
The Open Window/47

Com-mu-ta-tion

Pre-Dawn Dark/51
Ode to Brown/52
The Quilts of Gee's Bend, Alabama/54
Impressionism/56
A Study of Dust and Frogs/58
auGUST AUgust/60
Harlem Lines/62
Cambium Girl/66
Azzurro/68

Acknowledgments/71
Notes/75

To those so close beside me

John Hudson Couturier
Helen Margaret Merolla Poole
Helen Mary Breen

&

More than in memory of

Susan Park Poole Field
Justus Crossingham Poole

Bed of Crimson Joy

Backwards like the crab

Sister

A sliver of turquoise
the color of the veins
which once underwove
my sister's eyelids
presses apart the pink clouds
and the evening comes alive.

A heavenly shiver from the earth
moves up through my body.
The trees quiver with it, too,
tonight.

When my sister died
I clung to the autumn in her hair,
the humor in her eyes.
I dreamed I stroked the fiery hairs of her pubis
to bring her back to life.

But the dead go with the wind,
the abandoned breeze
that tickles young pin oak trees
on the nape, and they come alive.

Rembrandt's "Jewish Bride"

The couple glow as if
they were the only lamps left
in the loamy gloom of Amsterdam.
Though this is not a canvas
you would willingly enter,
not a bacchanal by Renoir
where you could slip in easily
between the pigments
among the round-bosomed women
and the bare-armed men and smile.

The bride and groom
do not look at each other.
What serious tenderness
in the placement of their hands:
his right hand flattened against her chest,
the other perched on her left shoulder,
the way he tilts toward her,
as if she were the only thing
to keep him from falling.

And it is true. Rembrandt
has made her the upright one
in the triangle their bodies form together.
She alone wears the smile of self-containment.
One of her hands rests lightly on his,
the other has fallen into the burning
folds of her dress. And the look
in her eyes reminds me of Anne Frank,
her whole life before her,
when she reached for her diary to write:
I still believe people
are really good at heart.

Bradford Pear Trees

These fruitless beauties mark the outbreak
of spring above New York's soot
and squalor. Their ghostly blooms lift up
even the hearts of lonely bums.
They thrive in poor soil, endure abuse
to the roots. Their flaw
is that their limbs are
brittle, too easily torn.

In childhood I worshipped symmetry
in my body: two hands
to play together, two legs to carry
me anywhere, and the eyes alike.
A year ago, when two rows
of Bradford pears bloomed on Saint Mark's Place
and I was falling in love,
my hopes roosted in the branches.

Tonight, I stand by the trunk of one
tree as if enclosed in my own
private planetarium. I know
how short-lived the tiny stars are,
like perfect moments, or dreams of children
and a well-planned life. But I am learning
about the joy in uselessness,
the beauty that can come from being barren.

Trees full of grace, forgive me my singleness:
the one heart that tips me over,
the one sexual opening that leads me astray,
and my mouth, lacking and insatiable,
awed, open.

The Urge to Pray in Bryant Park

Such single-pronged gleaming
the Chrysler Building gives off—
how I would like to genuflect under it
in this park swept of the derelicts
of twenty years ago, including me
then just starting out, a skinny
promotion assistant at Raven Press.

Neither single nor gleaming
I join the normal ones now
on rickety benches on the lawn
and like them tilt my face up.
The hole I was born with is getting larger.
Once I found a manger in there.
Now nothing. More and more of it.
So I've grown fat with dissatisfaction.

The Journey Home

It was the year I could only huddle,
bolt the apartment door and crawl
back to the closet for a sprawl among the shoes
that couldn't lead me anywhere anymore.

That year I abolished evenings and
afternoons to live in the eternal
dreamlight of kitchens—
my grandmother's luminous terrain.

I dreamed her by the stove about to hand me
toast to dunk in tea. I breathed in again
incense of her coffee. When I saw her image
in the garden, by the white Rose of Sharon,
tending the red roses in a circle of rocks,

something in her soothed me,
her stalwart, girlish shape?—
the way I imagine that Nausikaa soothed Odysseus
the morning after he was washed ashore.

He didn't know whether to stand
and face her or drop down on all fours
and beg. He stood and spoke beautiful words
so that she would help him get back home.

But I was speechless when my grandmother
came back in sleep to heal me. So she let me
sit, fully grown, on her lap. When I was ready,
she took my hands in her hands, and we danced.

Transcendentalists

For me, it's sausage sandwiches—
the half-stench, half-transcendent odor
of sweet ones and hot ones
mixed with the vapor of peppers and onions
as they cook toward translucence—
that bring back the night
I sailed into the sky on a Ferris wheel
with my father, the two of us dangling
carelessly over Little Italy.

We were having fun.
It was September. I was twelve,
my new breasts coming in
behind my pink preteen dress,
school not yet begun.

The wheel carried us into dark's
safe clasp. Our car stopped at the top
and rocked. When our heads fell back,
we swooned the way babies do
asleep in their carriages,
and it did not matter
that what we were
was not what we wanted to be.
We were lovers of little epiphanies,
prisoners of our goose flesh.

Jones Beach

On those afternoons when we swam in the Atlantic
my father went in in his tangerine
stretchy suit, a color that looked awful
against his pale, freckled skin.
My mother swam in a skirted, belted swimsuit.

She hated to get her face wet,
but we were powerless against the ocean.
The waves tumbled us to our knees
until we crawled out, sand heavy in our suits,
water tickling out of our ears,
warmer for having been inside of us.

At sunset we headed
for the avocado Rambler
my father had finally painted white.
Rolling all the windows
that would go down down
and leaving our underthings off,
we drove straight for McDonald's—
the breeze blowing inside,
sea salt still on our lips—
for the slender, languorous fries
and the mayonnaise and fish sandwiches.

All the while, my father's arm stuck out
the front left window
freckled and secure,
bent at the elbow
like a wishbone
with each of its two wishes still intact.

Swinging

When we took to the swings
of Claremont Park, the air
was darkening, the babies had all
gone home. And I, still daughter
not mother, wanted the three of us—
a family almost intact,
though no family is intact,
my sister dead twelve years,
the color of her hair having survived
in the leaves all around us—

to climb aboard those swings
and ride like mad.
Our six knees began to move in unison:
the freckled knees of my father,
high and delicate as my sister's,
the olive knees of my mother, swollen but still shapely,
and my own big-boned, vulnerable knees.
We began to pump. We began to fly.

Foal Days

During my foal days with grandfather
in his house by the Long Island Sound
the hydrangeas brimmed with bees.
We stood by the roses as
he lifted Japanese beetles
from scarlet petals
then dropped them in a Crisco tin of oil.

When we went down to the water,
I became a collector, carrying a musical pail.
I grabbed at the bellies of big,
glossy rocks, unsucking roan starfish
from their clutch.
I spent hours trying to coax
snails' feelers out.

He hardly spoke. The tide went
in and out. The sun sank
beyond the jetty. His stoic chest heaved
and fell. Dusk waved in the black pines.
I made coltish leaps over the tiny yews
before the stars came out
and he put me to sleep.

I was often too shy to kiss him
hello or good-bye.
The night he died of a stroke
I dreamed of a race—
who could pee the first—
and woke up entirely soaked with myself.
The second night, the spot was smaller.
I lay there guarding it
until it dried.

Adolescent Summer

In the unfinished attic of grandfather's
beach front house, we tried out makeup
in our black push-up padded bras.
Then we walked the bright stones
barefoot, climbing aboard pivotal
big rocks, the ones that marked
the tide's journey in or out.

We chose a black, barnacled
veteran to sit on all afternoon
as the Sound slowly surrounded us
until only the part of rock
on which we squatted was in the air.

We kept eating crispy chicken wings
and casting aside the bones,
letting the water douse us as it
licked at our seat.
Neither of us had yet been kissed.

Caught in Stone

The part of me never
held tightly enough
to anyone's breast
loosens on these
summer nights when
one leg thrown over
the sheet
I dream of women
on balconies
and fire-escapes
on porches and stoops
pausing the very moment
they decide to step out
into the humid
ceilingless night.

Tossed toward wakefulness
I remember the one aunt
who never married
who never gave birth
sleepwalker in her youth
and godmother to me
who if alive now
would be sitting
on her porch in the dark
staring out through the screens
her racehorse legs
bare and untouched
her cigarette tip orange
and crumbling,
my light, my firefly.

Every Day

My father walks down to the Hudson at 125th
where a few black men fish. He doesn't care
to fish. He likes his ramshackle turf; it's so good
for collecting old whiskey bottles and sardine tins.

My mother can't stand the collections he brings
home. On the sly, she throws his garbage out.
But when he says, "You are my memory,"
she is speechless, penitent.

He has forgotten people and places
and the stories he can still tell repeat and repeat,
his way of cutting a path
through tangled woods.

I retreat to when my father brought
Reese's cups home
or slipped a fresh orange
under my pillow when I lost a tooth.

He called me punkins. He gave me
a steering wheel that stood up in our car
right next to his. How seriously I
clutched it, mimicking every gesture as he drove.

Remembering Susan

Mute as it is, the earth is trying to say something,
or so I thought on Skytop Mountain, staring out at the hills,
mountains really, rippling off in every direction.

I thought the earth remembered. Not the way we remember
a particular person or thing. Larger than that, and impersonal.
As when light agrees to give memory a dress.

I couldn't help it. I began doing what we do.
Projecting my tortured cinematography upon them,
who were enough in themselves.

Susan's head come to rest in the nook of one crest,
held there the way we are held at the beginning if we are lucky.
I was. She wasn't, and she is invisible now and large,
more akin now to those mountains than to me.

Leave-Taking

The fog undoes the world tonight.
The landscape dissolves in it—
bitter lozenge.

Once out of the high-rise
I enter the realm of those
soon to disappear:

she with painful joints
and fading sight is easing now
into the fuzz of streetlamps;

he who says "I don't speak any English,"
an intelligent utterance from
a not-quite-right man, is quieted by mist.

Strange bliss when people diminish
and the weather takes over.
Those moments when suddenly

you are indistinguishable
from sky water rain.

In the Bedroom Under the Bookshelves

Like a tree bone smoothed by the sea
he lies adrift on the electric hospital bed,
a fine-boned and handsome mystery

who speaks now mainly through singing—off-notes
hummed, not *pianissimo,* into the chasm of air
that has grown fat by shrinking him.

In defense, he sometimes pulls a fast one.
Out of his mouth a matter-of-fact sentence comes full-blown,
all at once, before shortness of thought

loses the beginning or conveys the end beyond his reach.
I lift my pen to take down what he dictates,
but lose heart and wonder at the use.

Daddy is driftwood now and it doesn't
matter whether he knows my name.
His orphaned words form their own constellations.

And those much-loved tomes, read and unread on the shelves,
remain close to him, guardian angels,
with their wings closed.

Things—mutable as they are

Winter Light

It comes back to scuffed doorways and blackened windows,
to dusty floors and asphalt streets lodged with stars,
to the tops of the heads of commuters and beggars
as they ascend the subway stairs.
It stretches across slender bridges and broad ones,
travels along the bones of elevated highways,
down the trestle-legs, across the ramp-tails,
past neatly arranged houses in the suburbs,
their conformist yews and unprunable pines,
over abandoned warehouses, sweatshops, and graves.
It bounces off a child's flying saucer and neon snowsuit,
rests in the elderly, female crotches of the trees,
returns to the snow, whether unbroken or filthy,
to the pond frozen over and crowded on top with ducks.
It stumbles on lasting images of the dead: my sister's smile
the last time I saw her sane and alive, my aunt's post-surgical
expression, more dazed than joyful to have survived.
It comes back to the tense lover
suddenly smiling in his sleep.
Something in the light
remembers us
and radiance comes back.

Clear Night Outside Rite-Aid With Jupiter Overhead

I love that moment before it becomes
in little Leah's words
"really really really dark,"
and the sky turns slightly purplish
blue, when streetlights
that have stood sentinel
for years as I walked by
in my full spectrum of moods
begin coming on.
If then I cast my eyes down the wide avenues
and across the slim side streets—
space rising between the highest buildings,
as palpable for now
as the skyscrapers themselves—
I find myself caught for an instant
between the flesh and emptiness,
the cozy and the stark.

Music

Even at six
death worried me,
not my own
but the eventual deaths
of the others.
Playing the piano
induced a similar
gloom, though they praised
the way I fingered.
Such feeling.
And threatened me
with lifelong regret
if I gave the piano up.
But to bring music into being
made me feel too much.
I wanted to press my body
against the overwhelming sounds,
to exert my own small
counterpressure,
or at least to step inside
the music's delight
with one of the dance steps
I was learning—
glissade, assemblé, pas de chat.
Instead I sat there
stock still, my fingers stuck
in the sockets of the cosmos,
connected against my will
with the universe.

Hermes

He is the man you would leave home for.
I have seen his long legs poised,
his head atilt, the oblique look
of his eyes, the quiet loins, and wondered,
could he be waiting to take me away
or at least to receive me?

In Olympia, when I saw
the Hermes of Praxiteles,
I wanted never to come back
from that hip swung slightly
to the side, the pelvis ajar.
I'd seen him before, after waiting tables
at HoJo's, when I drove out to the shore
with the girls and the night cook
too tired and sweaty to sleep.

We had just slipped out
of our shoes and begun to cool
toes in damp sand
when the blond cook surprised us
by taking off his clothes.
Marbled by the moon,
he stood there without shame.
The others turned away.
I followed his flesh
along the sandbar, watched him thrash
unafraid through the undertow,
until he reached the deeps and dove in.

His was a beauty not above
but beyond fucking.
I had to drink it in:
flowing limbs, flowing torso.
For a moment, I was free
from struggle and work
and understood that this messenger,
a thief, was my muse.

Queen Anne's Lace

I am thinking of your penis—
the small made large—
and of the stubborn stem
of the Queen Anne's Lace,
a tough customer,
not to be unearthed.
Its flower begins
as an introverted nest
but when it opens I am privy to
the shape snowflakes possess
and fireworks strive for.

The Cockscomb

I admired your braggadocio, huge one,
shaped like a child's drawing
of the head of a tree, all your branches
lumped together—dark, puckery pink.
Cranberry ran in the veins
of your citron stalk. Under my hand,
your head felt stiff as pipe cleaners.
And your body, the more I looked, seemed
caught, born in the wrong kingdom: more fowl
than flower, eager to run off on proud feet.

I bought you, proud broccoli brains, because
you were definitely one of the more male flowers,
displaying your mohawk, your Elvis-do
no pistil and stamen heaven
for me to search for inside. On the contrary,
you honored the cock that rises
without our help throughout the night
and into the dawn, even in isolation
noteworthy, so showy, so alone.

The Camaraderie of Frogs

The pond sweetens me. Supple cattails
surround it, some upright, some bent down
by the wind, by the weight of a bird.
When I swam in its waters, I encountered
the cool currents of the parent stream,
though from the bank now
it looks quite still.

I obey that stillness, notice how each
bush and tree moves, is alive, even
the air through which a bee has etched
its halo of agitation above my head.

I am enjoying the company of two tiny frogs
that crouch next to me on their soggy reed.
Motionless, they keep watch over my shadow.
And at the splash of a fish,
I will share my thoughts with them because,
though lighter in aspect, they are as serious
as human thinkers in their own way.

The Cerebellum Singing Its Cosmic Scales

I am still a sucker for the sky.
For evening's azure negligée.
The pale-green canopy of spring—
bullet-ridden or lacy—
take your pick—
through which the dead
come and go at whim.
Feel them watch, brush past?
No amount of liquid tongue
can cling or clasp.
Yet these lines stack themselves
one by one, from the coccyx
of darkest matter to the spinal
cord of a thought.

Clark Gardens

I saw a crow so black
and secretive I lightened my step.
Beneath tall oaks, I heard
a sweet birdsong I didn't know.
I heard a peep by the still pond,
the muffled hum of a young bee,
the mechanical *chit chit, chit chit*
of a sprinkler.
I listened while a mother described
the metamorphosis of polliwogs to her young son
near the scummy skin of the pond.
And the sun began to calm me,
and I became giddy with the odor
of pine and rhododendron;
I gave up my fears and desires
for the dangling earrings
of crimson columbines.
I lay back and listened.
A mourning dove
moaned, and its song bore
the lull and drunkenness of summer.

By the Sound

Hold on
to my hair
with both your hands.
Love, let's be like
rocks sucked at by
water, black pines
loitering in sea air,
and unkempt magenta
beach roses.

Hummingbird Haiku

Ruby throat, come near.
Feed. Be punctilious.
Stitch, stitching sans thread.

Masculine / Feminine

Love-Charm Song

I come from the ocean.
I come ashore with foam trickling
  down my thighs.

The sight of me makes his soul
  and other parts rise up.
The sound of me makes him sing like a puffed
  red-winged blackbird in spring.
The odor of me reminds him of wet leaves
  on the forest floor.

When he touches my thighs
  he thinks of goose feathers.
When he kisses my lips
  he becomes lost in who he is,

so he can enter me.
so his whole body can go bare
  among the mosses and the fern fronds.
so he can understand why
  the oyster opens and closes.
so he can pass out of his body into the air
  and shimmer there for a moment
the way sun does on the water.

Floating Dream

I want to sleep with Rousseau's
sleeping gypsy, dream in the folded
rainbows of her dress,

watch her lion lover's
wide-awake eye in profile
rhyme with the full moon

and the itching stars
that climb through intricate
folds in her brain.

The sleeper clings
with her coal-black hand
to her walking stick.

Her pinky twinkles,
ignited by moonlight
in the scruff of his mane.

She has given up her lute
to the rough plucks of the wind,
her terra cotta vase to the stark desert air
that shocks and renews.

Things That Aren't There

When young, I loved
to press my eyelids
until colors came,
my first knowledge of the flesh star
that soars upward
through the body,
entering with such burning below,
you think you'll topple,
leaving through the top of your head,
a meteor burned to nothing
and your brain returned to loam.

For Vermeer and His "Sleeping Girl"

The room is drowsy with darkness.
Things are in disarray
but the girl sleeps on, sitting up:

Her cheeks flushed and soft
as the fruit in the bowl before her.

Her widow's peak cutting a heart
in her brow.

Her sturdy body beginning
to contain us the way the jug
in front of her has contained wine.

And the door to this room
always part way open.

So we go on wanting
what cannot be had:

To behold what her closed eyes see
without shuddering her awake.

The New Room

When I see the nervelike
beginnings of gingkoes,
something unknown in me sets off
up a tributary, entertains
leaving the ones I love.

I dream time after time of a new room
on the apartment, an undiscovered wing
I might grow into, huge
and full of light, with a view of trees
and sky. It saddens me to awaken.

It is death that grows, life that falls apart.
I live in a dark four and a half room walk-up.
My sister was a half-sister.
I hardly feel a pang now when I think of her.

My secret is the trees.
They let me go on when it was she
whose bare feet I had climbed upon,
she who smelled of autumn
and had autumn's apricot hair.

I have stood at her grave
a few long minutes,
felt great agitation in the air.
Though the elms above me remained peaceful
and the Ompompanoosac still pleased me
with its vowel-full name,
neither could soothe
the *Susan* in stone.

Orchidelirium

The women stare at the orchids much longer
than the men do,
as if the winged life within
were suddenly set before them,
not through reflection, without
mirror or lover,
but alone at last
for them to see.

And how should one approach the lips
of an orchid—
the blatant labia majora, the delicate
labia minora?
Some orchids are speckled and veined.
Each has the hill
of the clitoris at the top,
some are dragged by a pouch below.

How uniquely female: beauty
hovering around nothingness.
The word *sexy* on female lips
is an exhalation.

Watching the orchids in flower, I think
of the sad alleyway inside the word *cunt*.
In China, the vagina was an orchid boat.
Once I believed a woman might float on
her sexual eloquence forever.

Subway Flowers

You come home from the office
with ten fresh irises in your arms.
You bought them in the subway and
hold them out to me. I clip
the earthsides to let them drink.
All evening as we eat and talk
I sense their plump stalks
threatening not to open. In the morning
nearsighted, pessimistic, barely awake,
I tiptoe over to find
six inky buds have changed their sex,
become women now in indigo gypsy skirts
sliced to the waist.
I look down into the yolk-yellow sliver
that divides many of the petals.
I eye the buds that have stayed tight,
no gaffes or torn hems or slips showing yet.
How easily masculine and feminine
coexist in a vase.
I stay by their unfolding, not sure
whether I have slowed down or they are moving very fast,
whether their reaching for the space around them
mimics our hunger for each other
in miniature or blown up.
Last night, my menstrual body felt that
it could not be opened, but your heat
found its way
into that innermost place that is
unseeable, unnamable, seat of the imagination itself:
let's call it a cave,
let's call it land of the interior flowers,
let's call it night lake of reflected irises
waving their bodies wildly behind our eyes.

The Tightrope Walker Whose Wire Is Herself

In Rodin's sculpture of Iris
she is compacted into the smallest
space imaginable then opened from the center
like a sectioned fruit,
legs bent and parted, one knee northeast,
one knee west,
the pressed-open flower of her sex
reversing the tucked-in pelvis at prayer.

My iris has some of the hues of bruises.
Its petals dwell in the dangerous
bands of the spectrum I love,
where brightness fails and red orange
yellow green step down into blue indigo violet.

Virgin

It was not the man not the room not the night.
Say what it is, they say, about
being in beloved nothingness,
not nothing after all.
This is not Heidegger or Sartre
I'm talking about, but the vagina,
whose cave walls still glistened
with the barely dried images of bison,
which when he entered, whoever he was,
something like air rushed in,
altering the colors,
so no one would ever see those
animals quite the same way again.

Panic

Never-to-be-caught Now,
falter me. The reined-in horse
neighing, wide-eyed, made
to be still,
not happy yet closer, Now,
to you—to being alive.

Dear Anger,

get me past the girls' gate
beyond all that God-sap,
honey of sex flowing, heavy in their veins.

I'm moving beyond all I adored.
Come with Brutal Awareness.
Her value until now
I never understood.

Un

It was hard
I say
to continue.

My chute
of eggs emptied
one by one;

each went
unmet and
unnoticed.

Sorrow's ocean
dug steeper
declivities,

and I suffered hunger
and its under-
tow.

I was
unwary
and undone.

Un—the little
word part
became my mantra,

the magical pre-
fix meant to
undo time.

The Open Window

So much cachet in death and the moment.
But what of the moment when my mother says:
"Your father and I have come to the end
of our lives," and I realize she's ready to die,
wants it in fact, as relief from caring for
the rash on his buttocks, and the yelling
"You're going to kill me, kill me, kill me."
Then, "I love you, thank you, are you going
to take me with you?" All this recalled
before a paradise of color by Bonnard:
a cat, a woman asleep in the foreground
but out back, deeper in, a window open
to the forced-open blue cunt of the future.

Com-mu-ta-tion

1. A substitution, exchange, or interchange. **2.**a. The substitution of one kind of payment for another. b. The payment substituted. **3.** The travel of a commuter. **4.** Electricity. a. Conversion of alternating to unidirectional current. b. Reversal of current direction. **5.** Law. Reduction of a penalty to a less severe one.

The American Heritage Dictionary of the English Language

Pre-Dawn Dark

The body gets farther away.

And ego-bound, disappointing intelligence
is a brilliant fizzle
of a falling star.

Remember Dad's hand
clenched without rest
in the final year of his life?

I often find my own
in the same position—
fingers and palm concentrating.
Bearing down as much as any brain
on something
neither he nor I could
ever see.

Ode to Brown

Every morning they are still there
flanking the tracks:

brown limbs of the stick-figured trees
behind pin curls of barbed wire

pre- or post-figuring what?

The color they partake of now

> *Brown wanting to become gold*
> *but stuck in what it is*

goes with me into the gaze of
Dr. Cranendonk's radiating eyes
in the orgone therapy room years back.

> *Tiger eye. Tiger lily.*

Cranendonk, my gentle Thor,
six feet four with feet too long for shoes.

He'd been in the War,
the Underground,
and could say: *I was afraid.*

His large, warm hands
cradle my brain even now
when I think of him.

My express train flies through and past
the flit, glint, riff of life.
Nothing to hold on to.

These limbed inhabitants of earth are the place where nests appear and blend in. This brown is the color that seems to be background for something else until it alights like the goldfinch painted by Fabritius, a bird yellow, ochre, and brown that appears to flick its plumage within the small, still canvas. Fabritius died the same year he painted the bird. Killed in the Delft Gunpowder Explosion in 1654.

Note the brown noun-ness of the bare trees:
brown-gray-hideaway brown,
the color when the color in my hair begins to leave.

And the shadows of the trees
becoming more definite
than what they emanate from.

So how should I come at things?
With a slant or Eros's arrow?
Moot point as the arrow's already in

heart's lodge.
Hear the *dge dge* where the pain
meets the heart-thrump?

I swear I'll learn to swallow
my own tail,
be utterly economical.

The Quilts of Gee's Bend, Alabama

Start at the center.
Don't worry.
Your idea of what you're about to do
is going to become something else.

The colors will stare out at you—
having their say
in their own
quirk-ridden way—

patterns next to solids—
fainting lavenders
jutting up against cooling limes—

dungaree blues of a dead lover—
neighboring more dungaree blue—
pliant cottons and unwieldy cords
that bunched up—
refusing to lie flat.

You are going to make something to cover yourself with—
something to keep the kids warm—
something to lie under
made out of the dead, loved, worn-out, used-up-entirely-
in-this-life.

Because nothing is ever wasted.
We had nothing to buy anything with.
Lives were so hard.
*You wouldn't believe me if I told you
how hard our lives were.*

The torn fabrics will come together—
orange against white against black—
a little bit of cherry on the lower left:

no neat flowers in the quilting—
no tiny orderly squares
when you stand back.

The thread will leapfrog
wherever it wants to—
free to create arches and off-center webs:
star trails on which gazers can't help but stick.

Impressionism

I ride amid the
overwhelming ones—
airy bird songs
and swaying weeds

headlong into the field
of being itself

Because the dead
some of whom
I still love
live there—

perceived as fleeing
across this hayfield now

Leaving their willowy imprints
that let go their hold almost
as soon as they're made

Here and gone
here and gone
instantaneous
on the green

So when seen
from a distance
there is this slight
lag or lapse

between the impression
on the grass
and its release

which gives rise to a sheen
that moves
as if light and wind
were pigments mixed

Which is why
I said
willowy:

If you watch a willow
in the wind
you'll notice a half-beat

or more interval
between what
the willow limbs do

after what's done
to them
happens.

A Study of Dust and Frogs

No amount of showering can remove
the dust I feel settling on me now
at the end of the work day.

A cloud of fine, dry particles,
regarded as the result of disintegration
or the substance of the grave.

I stand alone with the herd at the White Plains
station as dusk goes deeper and dark birds—
are they crows—sail over and under the branches

reminders of essential things
I thought had to happen but never did.

A dispirited friend says *I feel*
nonexistent. Like a frog.
But frogs exist, I say.

Confusion, agitation, commotion.
Dust settling and unsettling.

Frog, frogs, just the word or thought of them
makes something in me perk up
something green, moist, magical
(I wanted to say vaginal).

Remember the frog odes Galway played
to break fledgling poets into song?

Remember the frog friend I longed for
as a child, not a prince, but the real wet-lipped thing
crouching and attentive, croaking and singing?

And then (hard to say to anyone)
there was the frog that came to the door
the night my sister died.

O dusty precepts of a bygone era.

The memory of her is of mistake
layered on mistake: psychotic break,
Thorazine, accidental overdose
not realized until it was too late.

Her shining-in-advance-of-everything
apricot hair never to be seen again
though some autumn trees take up her color.

Ashes to ashes, dust to dust.

That night by the orange lamplight of a country kitchen
I saw the frog's live body spread out
across the glass outer door
as translucent and veined as an umbilical cord,
the inside of him not separated from the outside of him

my faintly brown little man
come to tell me everything
yes, before it was too late.

auGUST AUgust

Nothing shone.
Even the trees limped
under such foliage.

And the implements
—rusty and large—
in the machine shops

whizzing past had no luster.
Words missing letters
offended the eye,

causing the proofreader's
brain to struggle—
what took so long

in forming
why take it
apart?

Then the solitary
sunflower
showed its face

amid the densation
of green

—*Ah, sunflower,*
you were my . . . weary,
alack

        clack clack clack
                      ek-
                            ko

of the woman on the train's wondering
how to remember
anymore
what you are.

Harlem Lines

I was riding a cement escalator above the ocean,
my hand talonlike on the rail,
cringing at the sight of that huge hospital
down there:
Earth.

I saw Highbridge Tower in the background,
the East River paralyzed, and the bridge at 132nd
diving in
head first.

All winter
the stream's black ink
wrote its way into the snow.

And I said to myself
So you think you're a wordsmith?
I'll polish your words
until you can see yourself in them.

Then a thought came to me:
we are ruled by miscellany.

There is an invisible nerve network out there
like secret writing it shows up when held
above the flame.

This is for the wacky conductor who told me
to look for dolphins in the Harlem.

Often the concept comes without the word.

The Wakefield owl I look for
every day on the west side of the train
is not an owl, not an eagle,
probably not even a peregrine falcon
but a red-tailed hawk.

My life's become the train
I can't remember my dreams:
In the morning, they're just
too feathered.

So I've taken interest in the plastic bags
caught by trees—their various
gestures, colors
always resemble something else.

The train takes a bold stroke
out over the ice-clumped river.
This week I will practice
how not-to-care.

Quick Lumber
Desabolladura y Pintura.

Well-wrought this wall: Weirds broke it.
The stronghold burst . . . .

Hitherto
only
effigies.

Effects (as in personal)
Things . . . the sad silly evidence of the things
as Shirley Hazzard says in *The Great Fire*

though, naturally, I'd prefer her other vein:
In those days, their bodies were taking
reciprocal shape, tentative, delectable.

Hitherto (the poems were)
only
effigies.

Gas Heats Best.
Freedom's in the air.
This hint of spring
is not suggestion.

The sweep of my life
keeps getting swept away.
So I have been dipping my hand
into death
like a bear
scooping at honey.

No Wakefield owl
today (or yesterday).

Goad—I look up the origin and come upon
spear, propel, prick.

Tuck-It-Away.
Gentleman's Cabaret.
Go-Go Girls (the meaning depends on
whether you want to stress
one *go* or two).
Sin City.

Masculine—the word itself
has a certain odor
musk-ox-like
though perhaps
not as heavy
as it seems.

Very like a bird
these tree limbs' shadows
when they stir.

Cambium Girl

Girl, who earlier
>   dreamed of ringlets
fat, brown slinkies down her back
and of the sophistication of wearing
>   slingback shoes,

Now has become this slim fish of a person
>   testing herself out
still too easily swallowed
>   by the deeps
or a field of tall reeds.

Her father called her
>   Long Drink of Water,
this frail changeling
>   to be returned to
for however many years
>   there are to come.

She was modeled on the tree,
whose writings are also internal:
>   tracings of
a single open vowel
>   O *o*
held, drawn,
echoed within itself

to mark time and protect
the living part of the tree:
        cambium,

Where cells divide
        and exchange themselves
for something tougher,
more useful:
        xylem or phloem—
though it is here
place of utmost passage

without which neither
she nor the tree
        could survive.

Azzurro

The sky reminded me today
of Italy,
except—no cupids.

Sometimes you want to be
something else—
the way the small black birds
sit at the ends
of the bare branches
pretending to be leaves.

As I stared at the clouds,
the desire came over me
to study Italian.
Una bella donna,
una ragazza dolce,
molti uomini—
all those vowels.

In Japan, the Shinkansen
bullet train
shot by the emerald rice fields'
immortal glistening.

And in Hiroshima, old and young
rode English racers—
la bicicletta,
un bosco oscuro.
It was a comfort—
their bike lights on in the dark.

Have you thought much
about the *bit*
in *ambition*—
the bit that wounds
and the bit that reins
wildness in?

Or about the words themselves
deserving homage—
submissive prisms
through which light unbraids itself
into colors
just passing through.

Acknowledgments

Grateful acknowledgment is made to the editors of the following print and online publications in which these poems appeared:

Ark: "The Journey Home"

The Black Fly Review: "Jones Beach"

Blue Mesa Review: "Hermes"

Bogg: "By the Sound"

The Bridge: "Caught in Stone" and "Every Day"

Ducts.org: "Panic," "Dear Anger," "The Cerebellum Singing Its Cosmic Scales," "For Vermeer and His 'Sleeping Girl,'" "The New Room," "The Tightrope Walker Whose Wire Is Herself," "auGUST, AUgust," "Cambium Girl," and "Hummingbird Haiku"

The Literary Review: "Sister" and "Transcendentalists"

Mississippi Review: "Rembrandt's 'Jewish Bride'"

Mudfish: "The Open Window," "Virgin," "Adolescent Summer," and "Foal Days"

New York Quarterly: "Love-Charm Song" and "Queen Anne's Lace"

Shenandoah: "Bradford Pear Trees"

"Azzurro," "Clear Night Outside Rite-Aid With Jupiter Overhead," "Harlem Lines," "Impressionism," "Ode to Brown," "Pre-Dawn Dark," "The Quilts of Gee's Bend, Alabama," and "A Study of Dust and Fog" were published in the anthology: *This Full Green Hour,* Sonopo Press (2008).

Thanks to artists/curators Tracey Munz Cataldo and Wendy Wolf, "Azzurro," "The Quilts of Gee's Bend, Alabama," "Clear Night Outside Rite-Aid With Jupiter Overhead," and "In the Bedroom Under the Bookshelves" were exhibited alongside paintings, photographs, sculptures, and collages in the Pearson Art Gallery's group shows.

This book was too long in the making, but it would never have become what it is without the generous help of numerous individuals at every stage.

Let me begin by thanking my kind and talented designer Nancy Figueiredo. Without her patience and skill the manuscript would never have become a beautiful bound book.

Thanks to the Edward Albee Foundation and the MacDowell Colony for granting me time to think, dream, and write in Montauk and Peterborough.

Thanks to the One O'Clock Poets—Guillermo Castro, Ron Drummond, Shira Dentz, Helen Ruth Freeman, Katie Johntz, Amy Lemmon, Katrinka Moore, Elizabeth Poreba, Martie McCleery Palar, Evelyn Reilly, Carly Sachs, and Sarah Stern for their poems and insights, which have fed my will to change.

Thanks to the trailblazing poets I met during my time at NYU, especially, Malena Mörling, Dana Levin, Alison Stone, Richard Tayson, Saskia Hamilton, Ann Keniston, Celia Bland, Mady Holzer, Sharon Krause, Gretchen Mattox, Joe Wenderoth, and Debra Weinstein. Their writings continue to inform and inspire my own.

Thanks to my teachers—Galway Kinnell, Jean Valentine, Sharon Olds, Colette Inez, David Ignatow, Robert Bly, James Hillman, Linda Gregg, Deborah Digges, Bill Matthews, Brenda Hillman, Marie Howe, and Stanley Plumly. I am better for having felt their hands working my poems.

Thanks to my tai chi teacher, Maggie Newman, who *is* poetry in motion. Her teachings and example have given me the courage to complete this book, and let it go.

Deepest thanks to my close friends, Helen Mary Breen, Carole Berruti, and Nathan Cabot Hale; my extended families, the Merollas, Fosters, Couturiers, Silvers, and Wilsons; my godson and most wicked critic, John Paul Foster; my makeup artist, Candy Rodó; and my loyal writer-buddies in publishing—Barbara Weisberg, Eileen Cowell, Don Gabor, and Jane Schwartz. They never let me let the flame go out.

Thanks to the young artist Emma Riba, whose impromptu drawing graces page 77.

Finally, my gratitude goes to my "without which I am nothing" supermom, Helen Margaret Merolla Poole, and to John Hudson Couturier, the editor's editor, who reviewed this manuscript in its various stages, more often than not suggesting a better word, phrase, or tack. Despite my initial resistance, I ended up listening to him more than to anyone else.

Notes

"Of those so close beside me . . ." is from "The Waking," by Theodore Roethke.

"The Jewish Bride," hangs in the Rijksmuseum in Amsterdam not far from Anne Frank House.

"Adolescent Summer" is for Kris Nelson Chandler.

"Clear Night Outside Rite-Aid With Jupiter Overhead" is for Leah Rose Silver.

In "Floating Dream," I was most likely mistaken about the gender of the gypsy.

When I revisited Vermeer's "Sleeping Girl" at the Metropolitan Museum of Art, I realized that the widow's peak I thought I saw might actually be just a hat.

The definition for *commutation* is quoted from *The American Heritage Dictionary of the English Language,* Fourth Edition (Houghton Mifflin Company, 2000).

"Ode to Brown" is for John Cranendonk.

"The Quilts of Gee's Bend, Alabama" is for the creators of these staggeringly beautiful quilts.

"auGUST AUgust" borrows snippets from "Ah, Sunflower" in *Songs of Innocence and Experience: Shewing the Two Contrary States of the Human Soul* by William Blake (1789 ° 1794) and "Sunflower Sutra" in *Howl and Other Poems* by Allen Ginsberg (City Lights Books, 1956).

"Harlem Lines" borrows several phrases from *The Great Fire* by Shirley Hazzard (Farrar, Straus, and Giroux, 2003) and from "The Ruin," translated by Michael Alexander in *The Earliest English Poems* (Penguin, 1966).

JOAN LAURI POOLE can often be found walking on Manhattan's East Side with a black miniature poodle. She was born into a family of music lovers. Her father worked as a record salesman for RCA and, on the side, played jazz and pop tunes on the trumpet. Her mother, a gifted classical pianist, ran the Merolla Music Shop on Long Island. Poole attended New York schools, from P.S. 125 to New York University, where she earned a graduate degree in creative writing. She makes her living as an editor and has also taught writing to undergraduates and elders. Generous selections of her poems have been published in the anthology *This Full Green Hour* and at *Ducts.org*. She lives with the poet John Couturier and the aforementioned dog, Oliver.

carrytiger

carrytiger is a small literary press devoted to poets, writers, and artists whose work has an essential strangeness and wonder that should be shared. The press takes its name from a tai chi posture, carry tiger to the mountain, which involves almost a half a turn. For more information, visit us at **carrytiger.com**.

Designer Nancy Figueiredo chose a digital version of the Bembo typeface for the poems in this book. Originally cut by Francesco Griffo in 1495, Bembo is named after the celebrated sixteenth century Venetian poet, diplomat, and philosopher Pietro Cardinal Bembo. It was first used to print Bembo's treatise *De Aetna,* about a visit to Sicily's famed volcano. Stanley Morison revived the font for the Monotype Corporation in 1929. Bembo is known for its cool, classical lines.

www.ingramcontent.com/pod-product-compliance
Lightning Source LLC
Chambersburg PA
CBHW031202090426
42736CB00009B/761